T0318461

Implementation of Total Quality Management

A Comprehensive Training Program

Implementation of Total Quality Management

A Comprehensive Training Program

Rolf E. Rogers, PhD, CMC

Routledge
Taylor & Francis Group
New York   London

First published by

International Business Press, an imprint of The Haworth Press, Inc., 10 Alice Street, Binghamton, NY 13904-1580

This edition published 2013 by Routledge

Routledge	Routledge
Taylor & Francis Group	Taylor & Francis Group
711 Third Avenue	2 Park Square, Milton Park
New York, NY 10017	Abingdon, Oxon OX14 4RN

Routledge is an imprint of the Taylor & Francis Group, an informa business

Library of Congress Cataloging-in-Publication Data

Rogers, Rolf E.
    Implementation of total quality management: a comprehensive training program / Rolf E. Rogers
        p. cm.
    Includes bibliographical references and index.
    ISBN 1-56024-996-X (hc: alk. paper)
    1. Total quality management. 2. Total quality management–Study and teaching. 3. Execu-tives–Training of. I. Title.
HD62. 15.R64 1996
658.5'62–dc20   ISBN 0-7890-0209-4 (alk. paper)   95-35018
                                                                                                                    CIP

CONTENTS

Preface   ix

Chapter One: TQM in America–A Review   1

Introduction   1
Manufacturing Industry   2
Auto Industry   3
Services Industries   7
Health Care Industry   9
Conclusion   12

**Chapter Two: Deming's 14 Points for TQM
Implementation**   15

Introduction   15
Deming's 14 Points   16
Possible Pitfalls Confronting Management
     in the Implementation of TQM   24
Conclusion   30

Chapter Three: TQM–Basic Concepts   33

TQM   34
The Chain Reaction for Quality Improvement   37

Chapter Four: Planned Organizational Change   39

Defining the Future State   40
Implementing Total Quality Management   41
Production Viewed as a <u>System</u>   42

Chapter Five: A Management Structure for TQM   43

Implementing the 14 Management Principles   45
Current Organizational Structure   46
Organizing for Transformation   49
Parallel Structure: Who and Function   52
Linking for Communication and Decision Making   59

Chapter Six: TQM Education and Training   63

Implementing the 14 Management Principles   64
Education and Training Strategy for TQM   69

Level I: Theory and Basic Concepts 70
Level II: Basic Methods and Tools 71
Level III: Advanced Methods 72
Courses 73

Chapter Seven: Organization Assessment **75**

What Is It? 76
Why Do It? 77
Functions of an Organization-Wide Survey (Generic) 78
When Do You Do It? 79
How Is It Done? 80
What Is Measured? 81
Who Participates? 82
Organization Climate Profile 83

Chapter Eight: TQM Implementation Guidelines **85**

**Chapter Nine: A Total Quality Management Process
Improvement Model** **91**

Implementing the 14 Management Principles 92
Purpose 93
Some Improvement Prerequisites 94
The Shewhart Cycle 95
Use of "Plan-Do-Check-Act" Cycle 96
Responsibilities During the Improvement Cycle 97
Process Improvement Model for Total Quality
    Management 98
Translating the Voice of the Customer 99
Process Improvement Model for Total Quality
    Management 100
Basic Graphic Tools 105
Continue the Cycle 107

Suggested Books and Monographs **109**

Selected Quality Management Journals **112**

Index **113**

ABOUT THE AUTHOR

Rolf E. Rogers, PhD, CMC, is Professor Emeritus of Management at The California Polytechnic State University, San Luis Obispo, California. He consults with the United States Navy on quality management, organizational assessment, team building, multicultural and cross-cultural factors on productivity, employee counseling, and sexual harassment prevention and education. Dr. Rogers has provided consultant services to numerous organizations in the United States, Canada, Australia, and the Middle East for over 25 years. He is the founder of Rogers & Associates, a management consulting firm specializing in organizational assessment and design, organizational and executive stress, cross-cultural sensitivity training and diversity management, total quality management (TQM), strategic planning, and sexual harassment education and training. His internationally respected work on organization, management, and behavior has been published extensively. Dr. Rogers is a Certified Management Consultant.

Preface

This book is designed to train the organization's workforce in Total Quality Management (TQM). Unlike other books on this subject, it provides a complete presentation from an introduction to the principles of quality management to a case application of implementing the concept. The presentation charts are arranged in sequential order and follow the approach used by the author in training seminars in the United States, Australia, and Saudi Arabia.

The introductory chapter presents a current overview of the status of TQM in the United States. This is recommended as a preliminary reading. The presentation charts have been generically designed to enable adaptation to different organizations. Unique characteristics, peculiar to specific organizations, can therefore be supplemented and added by the presenter as desired. A discussion of Deming's 14-Point TQM Philosophy has been included as Chapter Two.

The book assumes that the presenter has a basic understanding of quality management. The reference section lists many books on TQM principles which provide a helpful refresher for the presenter. Our purpose here was not to repeat the numerous discussions of TQM concepts contained in many available books but to provide a ready-made training format which can be used in all operational seminar/workshop contexts.

Rolf E. Rogers, PhD, CMC

Chapter One

TQM in America–A Review

INTRODUCTION

The legendary American quality consultant W. Edwards Deming, to whom the Japanese give credit for much of their success, was asked in a 1990 *Wall Street Journal* interview about the future of the American workplace. His answer: "What future?"[1]

Deming may or may not be a pessimist. In the last two years Japan has surpassed the United States manufacturing industry in productivity (output-per-man-hour). Japan's overhead as a percent of manufacturing cost remains the lowest of all industrialized nations. Japan's manufacturing overhead is nearly one-half that of the United States. Germany's overhead averages two-thirds that of the United States.[2]

These are just a few of the many reasons why America's manufacturing industry is finally waking up to the fact that their current managing techniques must change. Many American companies are starting to implement quality improvement programs as a way to ensure global competitiveness in the future.

It is no longer a matter of producing just "good" products and to compete only with American companies. To compete globally, our firms must produce quality products, using refined processes, managed by quality-conscious managers with quality principles. Increasing the focus on quality requires a long-term commitment

We wish to acknowledge the contribution of G. Douglas Lapp whose research was invaluable in developing this chapter.

and attention to detail. The result is a company that will be more responsive to customer's requirements, better able to sustain market share, and that will become more profitable.

The following text presents examples of how some American companies in both the manufacturing and service industries are currently implementing quality-improvement programs. Using Deming's 14 points as a prescription and incorporating more frequent use of workteams and flexible production throughout the company, remarkable results can be achieved. (See Chapter Two.)

· *MANUFACTURING INDUSTRY*

One quality implementation principle professed by W. E. Deming—his point number nine—is the need to break down barriers between staff and departmental employees. The objective is to integrate all departments of the firm. Barriers impede the smooth flow of processes. Defects and costs increase, and the customers (internal and external) are usually the ones to suffer.[3]

- This breakdown in barriers was one of the many techniques implemented by 3M in its St. Paul, Minnesota plant which helped to increase their profits. This same 3M plant also cut waste by 64 percent, customer's complaints by 90 percent, and increased production by 57 percent.

- Kodak has a quality program which enabled the company in one case to cut the defects in the plastic tips for its blood-analysis machines from 2,700 per million ten years ago to just two of the 600 million produced in the last four years.

- R. Heinz' Fremont plant implemented a quality program and with additional automation has received huge results in correcting the consistency of flavor and color in their catsup.[4]

Another positive technique to add to the quality-improvement program is that of workteams, both interdepartmental and intra-departmental. Communication throughout the company can be enhanced, resulting in process improvement. More important, however, is the fact that workteams are better able to break through creative blocks and achieve quality objectives at a faster rate with the company's best interest in mind. By empowering all workers and workteams to make decisions, not only can a firm eliminate unneeded middle managers and supervisors, but there is also the benefit of improved worker moral that results from the participation. This translates into more attention paid to the process, which yields more quality, increased production at less cost, and in turn, higher profits.

- Colgate-Palmolive Company's Hill Pet Products Inc. reduced cost and increased sales using flexible production and workteams at its Richmond, Indiana plant.[5]

With management and workers paying attention to quality at all levels of the production process, there is less need for quality inspection (control) at the final production steps. This is the essence of TQM. The seeds of quality are planted at the beginning of a product's life cycle and nurtured throughout the life span. Using this mind-set and employing necessary disciplines, a firm can better produce products that will compete in global markets.

AUTO INDUSTRY

Our nation's largest manufacturing employer, the auto industry, has been working to make improvements in the quality of its products over the last ten years. As is the case for companies in all industries, the total quality commitment must be incorporated into each firm's culture and ideology. The company must spread that obsession with total quality by making every manager, employee, supplier, distributor, and customer aware of the central position of quality in the product or service. Deming's point number one states, "Create a constancy of purpose for improvement of product and service."[6] The firm reiterates this commitment in its mission statement, short-term goals and strategies, and also with its long-term strategic goals and objectives. It is essential that top management make a total quality commitment.

- In 1980 Ford, GM, and Chrysler produced cars with three times the defect rate of Japanese cars. Defects here are defined as problems in the car's first 90 days out of the showroom. By 1990 they reduced this figure to reflect only 25 percent more defects than Japan.[7]

Cadillac Motor Division made dramatic reductions in their number of defects. This was undoubtedly one of the major reasons for winning the Commerce Department's Malcolm Baldridge National Quality Award in 1990.

- According to J. D. Powers and Associates, the California Market Researchers, the average car produced by the Big Three automakers has a 1.5 (per 1000) defect rate. That is down from a rate of 7 per 100 in 1981. Japan comes in with a 1.1 defect rate. In 1991 Ford Motor Company models actually averaged fewer defects than the Nissans, Mazdas, and Mitsubishis, but still lagged behind Japan's leaders Toyota and Honda.[8]

Teamwork in the Auto Industry

The auto industry, like other manufacturing industries, is using the team approach. Teams get involved in problem detection as well as making the decisions necessary to solve the problems and/or improve production processes.

There is a basic six-step problem-solving technique that can be adopted by worker teams:

1. Identify the problem and set a goal.
2. Analyze the problem.
3. Come up with as many potential solutions as possible.
4. Select what seems to be the best solution.
5. Implement the solution.
6. Try the solution for seven weeks. If it works, the problem is solved. If problems remain, go back to step 1.

- By adopting these exact techniques, GM turned its worst manufacturing plant in Buick City, Flint, Michigan, into its best. This plant makes the top-rated cars for quality of any U.S. manufacturer.[9]
- Teams of assemblers at Cadillac's Hamtramck plant in Michigan identified 300 problem areas on the 1992 Cadillac Seville. Teams of assemblers on one problem solution assignment were able to eliminate seven pounds of wiring.[10]

Simplicity

The Big Three are getting results in many ways. One is by just simplifying the operations at most plants. They use just-in-time systems, concurrent engineering, and thin-out technology-crammed operations to achieve the goal of creating lean and smooth-running processing plants. Simpler procedures leave less room for error.

A prime goal in all manufacturing plants is to reduce the cycle-time, or total time to produce one unit of a product.

- A team of metal-stamp press operators at GM's Grand Blanc, Michigan plant were able to cut the time it took to change the dies on certain presses from twelve hours to four and one-half minutes. This implementation also led to cost cuts by reducing inventory levels.[11]

The lack of concurrent engineering systems has perhaps been the American auto industry's costliest oversight problem. Using Deming's point number nine, "breaking down the barriers among departments" can result in numerous benefits for manufacturers.

The Japanese have been involved in concurrent engineering for 40 years. In concurrent engineering a team is developed from members of the supplier's marketers, engineers, and assemblers. This team gets involved in the project from the start, and by working together is able to save production time which in turn lowers cost.

The designs for manufacturing technique simplifies designs which in turn simplifies production. Quality design is the key to cutting product costs. While the cost of design represents only 5 percent of the average manufactured product's total cost, it affects 70 percent of total costs.

Design affects the material that may be used, the amount of labor needed for assembly, the complexity of production lines, and product reliability. Extra investment in design can result in big savings during production.[12]

- This simplifying process can help to reduce up to 25 percent of parts necessary per unit. Cadillac eliminated half the number of parts previously required when it redesigned the Seville's rear bumper system. Reducing the parts number from 130 to 63 helped reduce assembly time by 57 percent to less than eight minutes with an estimated annual labor savings of $462,000.[13]

Suppliers of industry are also incorporating the design-for-manufacturing in their own plants as well. This results in higher quality and lower costs of parts being passed on to the plant's assembly line, which eventually results in a higher-quality product out the door. Every firm incorporating this process should benefit.

- A large supplier of auto parts, Allied-Signal Corp's Sumpter, South Carolina plant, rebuilt their brake assembly line last year resulting in a reduction of defects by 86 percent and a doubling of production.[14]

American automakers have long been accused of being highly bureaucratic due to excessive middle management. This results in slower decision making as well as a slower turnover of new products.

- It takes an American firm 3 million man-hours to design a car ready for production as opposed to the Japanese 1.7 million man-hours. Detroit gets a new model to the public in 8 years whereas a Japanese firm takes only 4.5 years.[15]

SERVICES INDUSTRIES

There is growing evidence that quality programs are beginning to be introduced into America's huge and expanding service industries.

- While it is estimated that 10 percent of those in the service industry have begun some type of implementation, it is predicted that by the year 2000, 70 percent of the industries' members with 500 or more employees will be actively initiating some type of quality program.[16]

The tools and measuring techniques used when applying quality programs in the service sector can be quite different from those of manufacturing. The relationship a firm has with its customer is in many ways more personal or intimate than in other industries. But as in manufacturing, customer satisfaction is still the ultimate goal.

The products provided by service industry members such as

financial institutions, health care companies, airlines, and retailers are not always tangible in nature. In most cases it is the relationship that develops between the customer and the firm's employee, be it brief or for a lifetime, that constitutes the product.

According to Frederick Reichheld, founder and director of the consulting firm Buin and Company, the most valuable measure of a customer's satisfaction with the service business is favorable customer retention. This is basically the return business by satisfied customers. Reichheld indexes this return business as a retention rate. If a company consistently provides overall value (satisfaction) to the customer, the retention rate increases. An increase in customer retention results in increased profits. The logic here is that loyal, satisfied, returning customers actually cost less to keep than bringing in new customers. Most advertising, along with its cost, is aimed toward bringing in new customers. This results in lower margins with new—as opposed to existing—customers. Regular, loyal customers are also an inexpensive form of advertising when positive word of mouth is directed toward potential customers.

- Reichheld contends that a 20-year customer is worth 85 percent more in profits than a 10-year one. An increase of 2 percent in retention rate has the same effect on profits as a 10 percent cut in cost.[17]

Training and education of employees in customer service and product orientation is a step that all service businesses need to be engaged in. Of Deming's 14 points, point number 13 may be the one required the most when it comes to a serious implementation of a quality program by service companies.

This point states the need to institute a vigorous program of education and self-improvement for all employees. This is intended for all members of the organization. Deming also believes that this step, and all steps, need to be continually practiced.[18]

- Federal Express package sorters are tested every three months for accuracy. Anyone who fails to meet the criteria is sent for retraining.[19]
- Marriott Corp. has put 70,000 of its hotel employees through empowerment training courses. The course stresses the need for employees to make their own decisions pertaining to customer problems, since they are the ones in contact with customers.[20]
- University Microfilms Inc., a Bell & Howell subsidiary in Ann Arbor, Michigan, has spent $1.5 million since 1988 to put its 1,000-plus employees through quality training courses.[21]

HEALTH CARE INDUSTRY

Private sector employers and the government spend over $670 billion annually on health care. Pressure to lower cost and increase quality in this growing industry is on the increase from employers and insurer groups. Defining what quality means in health care is not significantly different from other organizations. Consistency in care is definitely what customers today are seeking.

- One study by General Electric Corporation in 1988 showed that their employees in Utica, New York were getting more attention in surgical procedures than those employees living 50 miles away in Syracuse.
- Companies such as B. P. American, Parker Hannifin, and Reliance Electric are working together with 30 area companies in Cleveland to devise a hospital quality ranking system.
- Interstudy, a health policy think tank in Minneapolis, is compiling a national data bank to track the treatment of mil-

lions of patients. Data comes from large employers such as AT&T, Marriott, and Ameritech. What is being called an "accounting system" for medicine will allow physicians to see how patients respond to different treatments and allow patients (consumers) to compare physician performance.[22]

The operation of a hospital is beginning to be viewed by its managers as though it were like a manufacturing plant. It is a complex production center with a multitude of "processes." The "customers" are the patients and purchasers of care (the product). Laboratories, surgeons, and nurses are the "suppliers." Quality depends on the coordination of departments and employees. Cooperation among such a variety of interdependent groups is essential to providing consistent quality care.

The Chairman of the Juran Institute Inc., A. Blanton Godfrey, started the National Demonstration Project on Quality Improvement in Health Care. This group is conducting a year-long experiment in the application of quality programs for the health care industry. Experts in quality from Ford, Xerox, and Hewlett-Packard were teamed up with members from 21 health care providers to address perceived problems in the industry. The project teams did not analyze actual medical staff. Their attention was mostly focused on hospital functions such as discharge, housekeeping, and food services.

- One project team at the University of Michigan Hospital focused on patient admittance. By reorganizing the admittance staff, a process that once took 2.3 hours was reduced to 11 minutes, resulting in a yearly cost savings estimated at $260,000.[23]

There are currently steps being taken by both the American Medical Association (AMA) and one of the nation's largest health management organizations (HMOs), U.S. Healthcare Inc., to help doctors improve their care provision. The AMA is setting the parameters for its members in providing the available care, and Healthcare Inc. is beginning to survey their subscribers annually about care received in an attempt to bring consumerism and accountability into health care. They also link physician pay to the quality of care.

- A 99 percent defect-free rate in the healthcare industry would be a nightmare. Most manufacturers, from computer chips to electronic parts, shoot for a defect-free target of 99.9999998 percent. According to Liggett Stashower, quality control executive for Motorola, "With only 99 percent performance rate, hospital workers would accidentally drop 30,000 newborn babies each year."[24]

Intermountain Health Care Inc. (IHC) is the leader among hospital chains with its clinical application of quality management techniques, according to Stephen Shortell, a professor at Northwest University. He is currently surveying 6,000 hospitals in an attempt to see how many are implementing quality programs and to what degree. IHC adopted quality principles throughout their 24 Utah hospitals. Their aim was to find and eliminate intolerable variations in medical care provided by staff nurses and doctors. IHC conducted an experiment at one of its bed hospitals in Salt Lake City in an attempt to lower postoperative wound infections.

They once had an infection rate of 1.8 percent. By paying more attention to their patients and using computers to aid in the dispension of antibiotics before operations, they now have a post-operative infection rate of 0.4 percent, down 25 percent from the start of the experiment.[25]

The Executive Director of IHC's Institute for Healthcare Delivery and also their quality chief, Dr. Brent C. James, is working toward a reduction of up to 60 percent of medical mistakes which could reduce per hospital cost by as much as 2 million dollars a year.[26]

CONCLUSION

We are in a new economic age. We can no longer live with commonly accepted levels of mistakes . . . . We have learned to live in a world of mistakes and defective products as if they were necessary to life. It is time to adopt a new religion in America.

W. Edwards Deming

America is about to come back. "Made in the USA" will become a symbol of world-class quality again. When 30% of US products were failures, vs 3% for Japan, that was an enormous difference. But at failures of 0.3% and 0.03%, it'll be difficult for anyone to tell the difference.

J. M. Juran

American industries are capable of producing quality products and services that can compete globally. Many companies nation-wide are implementing total quality programs with impressive results. The American worker is still the most productive in the world. It is true that the U.S. has a lot of work ahead. America must not neglect the education of its people if we hope to retain or improve our standard of living. With a sense of concerned optimism, America will persevere in these difficulties.

REFERENCE NOTES

1. *Boardroom Reports,* "Deming on the American Future," p. 5, December 1, 1990, taken from the *Wall Street Journal,* June 1, 1990.

2. *Business Week,* "The Quality Imperative," p. 66, October 25,1991.

3. Gitlow, H. S. and Gitlow, S. J., *The Deming Guide to Quality and Competitive Position,* (1987), p. 140.

4. *Business Week,* October 1991, *op. cit.*, p. 66.

5. *Business Week,* October 1991, *op. cit.*, p. 66.

6. Deming, W. E., *Out of the Crisis,* (1986).

7. *Business Week,* October 22, 1990, p. 84.

8. *Business Week,* October 1991, *op. cit.*, p. 70.

9. *Boardroom Reports,* "Buick's new quality secrets."

10. *Business Week,* October 1991, *op. cit.*, p. 71.

11. *Business Week,* October 1991, *op. cit.*, p. 71.

12. Huthwait, B., President, Institute for Competitive Design, speech originally published in *Purchasing*, reprinted in *Boardroom Reports,* June 1, 1990, p. 2.

13. *Business Week,* October 1991, *op. cit.*, p. 73.

14. *Business Week,* October 1991, *op. cit.*, p. 72.

15. *Business Week,* October 1991, *op. cit.*, p. 72.

16. *Business Week,* October 1991, *op. cit.*, p. 100.

17. *Business Week,* October 1991, *op. cit.*, p. 102.

18. Gitlow, *op. cit.,* p. 182.

19. Liswood, L., "Serving them Right," *Boardroom Reports,* September 1, 1990, p. 2.

20. *Business Week,* October 1991, *op. cit.,* p. 100.

21. *Business Week,* October 1991, *op. cit.,* p. 101.

22. *Business Week,* October 1991, *op. cit.,* p. 111-112.

23. *Business Week,* October 1991, *op. cit.*, p. 112.

24. Industry Week quote from *Boardroom Reports,* November 15, 1990, p. 16.

25. *Business Week,* "The RX at Work in Utah, October 25, 1991, p. 113.

26. *Business Week,* "The RX at Work in Utah,*" op. cit.* p. 113.

BIBLIOGRAPHY

"Auto Quality," *Business Week*, October 22,1990.

Boardroom Reports, June 1, 1990.

Boardroom Reports, September 1,1990.

Boardroom Reports, November 15, 1990.

Boardroom Reports, February 1,1991.

Crosby, P. B., *Quality Is Free: The Art of Making Quality Certain.* New York: Mentor Books, 1990.

Deming, W. E., *Out of the Crisis,* Cambridge, MA: Massachusetts Institute of Technology, 1986.

Gitlow, H. S. and Gitlow, S. J., *The Deming Guide to Quality and Competitive Position*. NJ: Prentice Hall, 1987.

"Innovation in America," *Business Week* Special Issue, January 1,1990.

"The Quality Imperative," *Business Week* Special Issue, October 25,1991.

Rogers, R. E., *Total Quality Management: A Proposed Model for Establishing Quality Criteria and Measuring Performance Under TQM*. San Luis Obispo, CA: California Polytechnic State University, 1992.

Scott, W. G. and Hart, D. K., *Organizational Values in America*. New Brunswick, NJ: Transaction Publishers, 1990.

Chapter Two

Deming's 14 Points for TQM Implementation

INTRODUCTION

W. Edwards Deming's 14-point program constitutes the core of his recommendations for achieving quality excellence through continuous improvement. While each point can be addressed separately, it is the synergistic implementation that will provide a total quality management focus for the organization. His philosophy places the responsibility for quality improvement in the hands of management as well as in the hands of the employees. For many organizations, this philosophy forces radical changes in management approaches and work processes. It requires a complete reassessment of past and present modes of operation. Numerical goals, quotas, and incentive structures will have to be changed or even eliminated. Organizations must develop new policies of supplier relationships, cultivate intolerance for defective materials and services, and start significant new training and education programs. All of these activities will create major changes in the organization, the relationships between mangers and employees, the work process, and the relationship with the customer.

We wish to acknowledge the contribution of Shawn Tackitt whose research was invaluable in developing this chapter.

DEMING'S 14 POINTS

Point 1: Create constancy of purpose toward improvement of product and service.

The American management system has become overwhelmed by the day-to-day issues that demand attention in order to survive for tomorrow. The adoption of this short-term view has only complicated the process that it will take for TQM to be successfully implemented. The short-term view is analogous to the many programs that are installed to fix immediate, reactive problems. TQM must be viewed as a long-term process, continually looking into the future. Organizations will not only have to meet short-term requirements, but plan for their existence in the future.

The process of (1) developing a mission statement, (2) making it a living document, and (3) socializing new employees to the mission statement is what is needed to begin the "journey to quality."[1] The development of such a document needs to include input from employees, stockholders, management, vendors, and the customers. This document is the "guide" for the organization to meet future goals, and should be treated as such. It should be read and constantly updated as goals change to meet future requirements.

The mission statement and organizational philosophy must be believed by management as well as the employees. A consistency of purpose must be created and followed to effectively meet organization goals. Unifying goals is the first step toward making decisions in a consistent manner, in order to provide stability and confidence for the long-term view.

Point 2: Adopt a new philosophy.

Many American managers are managing for failure instead of managing for success. A new philosophy must be adopted, one that may be contrary to the current culture of the organization.

Quality-conscious attitudes will have to replace existing short-term survival practices. This process will not be easy; fear is often created when one moves from the status quo to the unknown. To overcome this fear, the move will have to include everyone in the organization.

To facilitate this move to the unknown, certain variables will have to be defined. In the past, error was regarded as inevitable, acceptable, and even a means of measuring profits. Perfection should be the only standard to achieve profits; therefore, quality must be defined. Once quality is defined, consistency can be achieved, enabling the organization to move ahead toward continuous improvement.

With quality defined, the organization can move from defect detection to defect prevention. The only acceptable costs of quality are (1) the costs of preventing errors and creating error-free designs and (2) the expense of developing training programs in quality awareness, problem-solving skills, statistical process control, and responsiveness to customers.[2] Given time, total quality will cost less as production time is reduced, back orders decrease, and customer complaints lessen.

Point 3: Cease dependence on mass inspection.

Making it right the first time is the answer to mass inspection. Mass inspection is part of the short-term view: implying that organizations intend to make defective products. The biggest problem with mass inspection is that it occurs after production. Resources have already been used to produce a product that does not conform to defined standards. Another problem with mass inspection is that it is not without error. Often it is performed under pressure, which increases error. The result of inspection is only short-term. There are generally no provisions for the identification of problems, improving the process, or achieving higher quality.

Point 4: End the practice of awarding business on the basis of the price tag.

Purchasing must be based on quality as well as price. In today's marketplace, this calls for purchasing agents who can judge quality. An important criterion for meeting today's demand for quality is that the purchaser must understand how each part fits into the total system. If possible, the purchase should be followed all the way to the customer. This will provide the greatest insight toward providing quality that exceeds the customer's needs.

Purchasing on the basis of price alone has lead to the commonly accepted practice in the United States of multiple vendor relationships. This practice is in direct conflict with Deming's concept of a long-term view. Relationships need to be built with vendors to provide continuous improvement for the long run. By purchasing from multiple vendors, the quality support decreases, resulting in decreased vendor responsibility. There are also increased costs when dealing with multiple vendors. Costs include: increased travel expenses to visit vendor facilities, increased paperwork, increased telephone expenses, loss of volume discounts, increased set-up charges, increased investment in capital equipment and/or test equipment that must be provided to the vendor, and increased inventory costs due to carrying multiple vendors' items and their spare parts.[3]

Point 5: Continual improvement of the system.

Improving the system will begin with precise definitions of specifications, products or services, and jobs. Using defect detection is managing for failure. The long-term view calls for a movement toward defect prevention.

The system needs to go through continual improvement to stabilize variation. As variation decreases, quality will improve the system not only internally, but externally as well. Vendors need to be constantly involved in the improvement of the system. Definitions and specifications need to be readily conveyed to increase stability.

Point 6: Institute modern methods of training on the job.

Training must be viewed as a continuous approach toward increasing the growth and development of the employee. Too often, training is used as a reactionary response to a new problem facing the organization. Under Deming's philosophy, the employee is the organization's greatest asset. Thus the organization that commits to a long-term view will realize that its employees hold the keys toward reaching goals.

A traditional approach to training newly hired employees is to attach them to an experienced worker in the belief that the new employee will learn by osmosis. There are several problems with this method, for example: the experienced worker may not be a good teacher; time pressures may force the new worker to produce before being completely ready; the experienced worker may omit some explanations because of being so accustomed to doing the job; and the trainee may learn only the particular job task.

Management needs to view training as everyone's job in the organization. With input from all levels of the organization, needs can be assessed and training programs can then be implemented. It is important for the employees to understand where they fit into the process, in order to function as part of the long-term view. The most important part of any training is evaluation after the training has been completed.

Point 7: Institute modern methods of supervision.

As part of the long-term view, management needs to build a specific relationship with its employees. In order to develop this relationship, management needs to play a more supportive role, focusing on the positive aspects of the individual employee. Once this relationship is established, the employee will be more open to both praise and constructive criticism. Deming states "The aim of supervision should be to improve the performance of man and machine, to increase output, and simultaneously to lighten the load of the production worker, to make his job more interesting as well as more productive."[4]

These long-term perspectives can clearly be achieved with new approaches to supervision. Implementing control charts to track performance not only illustrates a clearer picture of overall employee performance, but also enables the employee to see increases and decreases. Management commitment to better training also helps facilitate better supervision; as training increases, employees feel better about the job they are doing. Knowing where each employee's job fits into the big picture also instills a sense of pride in workmanship. As quality is further emphasized, it also will have the effect of moving down the levels of the organization to further emphasize the process of continuous improvement.

Point 8: Drive out fear so that everyone may work effectively.

If a long-term view toward continuous improvement is to be successful, then fear must be driven out of the organization. Elements of fear can include: lack of job security, possibility of physical harm, performance appraisals, poorly defined company goals, inadequate training, and quota systems.[5]

Top management needs to provide an atmosphere that is inviting and secure for its employees. As relationships are established, this atmosphere becomes increasingly easier to obtain. The relationship will stem from management's ability to provide the workers with adequate training, guidance, and the necessary resources to do the job correctly. Once fear has been removed, employees and management will be able to work together to meet and exceed desired goals.

Point 9: Break down barriers between departments.

Breaking down barriers is paramount to the long-term perspective. Driving out fear and providing adequate training will go a long way toward the reduction of obstacles but time must be given to completely purge an organization of established barriers. Management must lead the way in changing attitudes to meet the requirements of the new philosophy of constant improvement to quality.

Barriers are created for a variety of reasons, but communication, or the lack of it, seems to lie at the root of this problem. Communication is the basis for relationships, and once communication is established employees can begin to trust each other. As trust and cooperation increase, barriers within the organization will begin to decrease. Structuring teams within organizational departments is also helpful in reducing departmental barriers. Team building promotes camaraderie and bonding as members rely on each other to solve problems.

Point 10: Eliminate numerical goals, posters, and slogans that seek new levels of productivity without providing methods.

Numerical goals, posters, and slogans are worthless unless employees are provided with the tools to achieve management's desires. Deming states that "goals are necessary for you and me, but numerical goals set for other people without a provision for a road map to reach the goal, have effects opposite to the effects sought. They generate frustration and resentment. The message that they carry to everyone is that management is dumping their responsibilities onto the work force."[6]

The first goal established should be the goal of continuous improvement of quality. All goals stated thereafter should be in quality context. As workers begin to understand how they fit into the goal, tensions, fears, and resentment toward management will decrease.

Point 11: Eliminate work standards that prescribe numerical quotas.

Work standards and quotas only consider quantity, with little regard to quality. Work standards and quota systems are tools of the short-term view, and must be eliminated to achieve continuous improvement of quality. Work standards and quotas also destroy employee morale, motivation, and pride because they encourage defects to meet the quotas. The result of implementing work standards and quotas is managing for failure; no one prospers.

Communication declines under work standards and quota systems. These systems symbolize management's lack of commitment to the long-term view. Fear is also instilled as employees are unable to reach high quotas, further deteriorating management-employee relations. The consumer is also affected by the work standards and quota system. Defects rise as a result of trying to meet quotas, thus causing productivity to decrease and costs to rise as products are reworked. The consumer is subjected to higher prices that could have been avoided.

Point 12: Remove barriers that rob employees of their pride of workmanship.

There are several reasons employees lose their pride of workmanship. Implementing poor training programs is one. If employees do not know what is expected of them, they cannot accomplish their jobs. Pride is lost by employees who are not provided with adequate tools. There are others, but the majority stem from the organizational system itself.

Implementing the long-term perspective, and viewing employees as valuable assets to the organization helps instill pride of workmanship. Creating constancy of purpose in the organization, and educating the whole organization to the goals and mission statement also help employees identify their part in the big picture. Removing the barriers that hinder employee pride in workmanship will facilitate the movement of decision making down to the lowest possible levels. This enables supervisors to become "leaders" and "facilitators" of the long-term view.

Point 13: Institute a vigorous program of education and retraining.

Training and educational programs are critical to the success of the long-term view. Training and education programs provide the employees with the means to maintain a competitive edge in a continually changing market environment. Training and education provide the organization with the road map to achieve continuous improvement. The key to success is to provide customers with products that they have not envisioned. Without educational and training programs, this cannot be achieved.

Training must start with the new philosophy of continuous improvement. Once a constancy of purpose is achieved in relation to the organization's mission statement and goals, further training can continue. Everyone in the organization will need to be trained in statistical operations. This is necessary for the implementation of the new methods brought about by continuous improvement. Training also will need to be done in basic areas of math, reading, and both verbal and written communication. It is important that everyone can understand and communicate well with each other to meet organizational goals.

Point 14: Create a structure which will push on the prior 13 points every day.

Top management is responsible for providing the tools and techniques for employees to achieve the goals of continuous improvement. Providing these tools and techniques means a strong commitment to living the philosophy. Time must be given to achieve the established goals and to continue to strive for future improvement. To facilitate the tools and techniques, managers, quality committees, and workers' quality teams will have to be established. Starting at the top, information can then be passed both up and down to provide continuous feedback on quality improvements.

POSSIBLE PITFALLS CONFRONTING MANAGEMENT IN THE IMPLEMENTATION OF TQM

1. Meeting Present and Future Challenges

Management must not only facilitate methods for dealing with today's problems, but also provide insight for future problems. Failing to foresee future problems is failing to meet tomorrow's needs. Management must continually plan for future development in the following areas: customer needs and performance requirements, products and services, materials, methods, training and skills requirements, supervisory methods, cost of production and marketing, etc.[7]

The mission statement is a "living" document. It is a guidance tool representing the overall corporate philosophy, and should be treated as such. It is everyone's responsibility to make sure that the statement remains alive within the organization. A philosophy is only a set of beliefs, not an answer to every problem that might arise in the organization. Treating the mission statement as if it were cast in stone only causes inflexibility. To meet present as well as future challenges, organizations will need to remain flexible.

2. Lack of Management Responsibility to Support Removal of Barriers

Many people in the organization will want to resist the change to the long-term view. They will feel that they have survived and even prospered under the old system, and exhibit a reluctance to change. Top management must be involved in helping remove these fears, conveying support to lower-level managers and employees. It must be management's responsibility to encourage the removal of barriers toward the new long-term view.

Another pitfall associated with point two of Deming's 14 points is management's inability to properly define quality. Quality must be correctly defined to continue on the road to improved quality. Quality is defined in terms of customer needs and expectations. Without knowing the customers' needs and expectations, the product quality only meets company expectations. This would be fine if the company were the customer, but it is not.

3. Failing to Remove Factors that Limit Quality

Implementing Deming's philosophy relies on both humanistic and statistical aspects, and both are necessary for success. Deming believes that in order to achieve quality, statistical methods must be employed. Abandoning mass inspection and moving toward defect detection requires precise quantitative data. This data can only be adequately obtained through the use of a statistician.[8]

In addition to removing factors that limit quality in the organization, communication with vendors must be established. Just as the organization defines quality based on customers' needs and expectations, the organization is the vendor's customer. It is the organization's responsibility to convey vital information to help improve the vendor's process as well as its own.

4. A Reluctance to Transform from Multiple to Single Vendors

A pitfall associated with point four of Deming's 14 points is inadequate training and supervision of purchasing agents. The purchasing function must be incorporated into the long-term view. Knowledge in the areas of statistical methods and vendor relations will be a requirement. Without proper supervision in the transformation from short-term purchasing practices to long-term, purchasers will continue to purchase the old way.

Management must not resist purchasing from single vendors. This does not mean the move to a single vendor must be made overnight. A transition will be required to move from multiple vendor purchasing to single vendor purchasing. To achieve this transition, management must be educated in the benefits and provide support to the organization in order for it to be successful. It will be important for management not to send double messages to purchasing agents. If there is a true commitment toward the long-term view, then purchasers must not be influenced in making quality-focused purchasing decisions.

5. Failure to Provide a Supportive Atmosphere

One pitfall associated with improving the system is management's inability to provide an atmosphere that is supportive of the new tasks the employees will be required to perform. Step five will call for employees to learn statistical methods to help reduce variation in the system. Without proper support, employees will abandon the use of these methods.

The implementation of the new methods associated with quality improvement must be slowly introduced into the organization. Quality, productivity, and competitive position cannot be achieved by massive, immediate use of control charts and other statistical techniques by hourly workers. Anyone who supposes that will doom his own career and carry his company along with him.[9]

6. Management's Failure to Provide Adequate Training

Some employees will naturally resist the new types of training that support the new philosophy. It is management's responsibility to help the employees to make a smooth transition toward the new philosophy. Management will have to provide the proper tools and techniques for employees to be trained in the new methods of continuous improvement. Training will have to be viewed as a continuous process, constantly being refined. Refinement will be required both for the employees and the trainers.

7. Failure to Maintain Lines of Authority

Under the new philosophy, lower-level managers tend to feel insecure about the level of authority they will have under the new system. The new system calls for a more supportive approach to management, with a high focus on teamwork. Although teamwork is a very important part of the new system, lines of authority must exist. Management must emphasize this issue, and be ready to support its views if challenged.

The long-term view calls for a more humanistic approach toward the supervision of employees. Management will have to learn to support employees, viewing them as important assets in the organization. When personal problems arise, the employee should not be penalized for unforeseen circumstances. Management also must create new performance appraisal systems to support the new attitudes toward employees. Using the old performance appraisal system will be dysfunctional. A new appraisal system, based on teamwork and quality, must be established.

8. Lack of Organizational Communication

Deming feels that "the fundamental problem in American business is that people are scared to discuss the problems of people." Management's job is to deal with employee problems, fears, and development. A cautious approach must be taken in the monitoring of fear. Believing that fear has been eliminated when it still exists can be devastating to the implementation of the long-term view. Establishing relations and communication channels is the only way to determine if fear has been totally removed from the environment.

Furthermore, not planning for the new fears that the long-term view will create is also managing for failure. Concentrating on driving out the existing fears is only the first step. Fears of mistrust, security, and insecurities in communicating must all be dealt with in the same manner as existing organizational fears.

9. Denying the Existence of Barriers

Management must no longer deny that barriers exist in an organization. Every organization has some degree of barriers. The issue is to what degree. Many times barriers are so big, and have been established so long, that working without them is nearly impossible to contemplate. Management must take the responsibility to honestly evaluate the levels of barriers that exist, and take the proper actions to eliminate them.

Once barriers have been identified, management must not send double messages, by allowing the elements that create barriers to continue to exist, (e.g., privileges and separate facilities). Management must also appropriately deal with employee resistance to eliminating barriers. Many employees have worked with and even benefited from barriers for long periods of time. As a result, resistance and even sabotage may meet management's attempts to eliminate barriers. Failing to identify and help these employees will be disastrous to the long-term view.

10. Failing to Evaluate in Terms of Quality

Continued reliance on posters and slogans is a detriment to the success of the new philosophy. Management must not allow the use of these techniques, and must make sure that they are truly eliminated. The new philosophy will need to be evaluated in terms of qualitative accomplishments versus quantitative measurements.

Management traditionally has relied upon numerical goals because it holds the erroneous notions that these: (a) let individuals clearly know what is expected of them, (b) improve communication between supervisors and subordinates, and (c) are needed as motivators to keep people on "track."[10] Failing to trust qualitative goals rather than quantitative goals must be eliminated in order to begin the journey toward continuous improvement.

11. Clinging to the Short-Term View

One common pitfall in implementing point 11 of Deming's 14 points is clinging to the short-term view. Believing that the current work standards and quotas are the best that can be achieved will be the death of the long-term view. Management must change these beliefs if the company is to be successful in the long run.

Before the elimination of work standards can be accomplished, management must trust the ability of the long-term view to eliminate the need for work standards and quotas. The trust must also be present in the rest of the organization; if implemented too soon, it will be met with certain resistance.

12. Inability to Become Leaders and Facilitators

Trying to instill pride by inappropriate methods is often a pitfall associated with point 12 of Deming's 14-point philosophy. Methods that include slogans and posters, fear, discipline, and quantitative measures are all inappropriate under the long-term view. Management must realize that these methods must not be allowed to exist in an organization that is seeking total quality improvement.

The inability of management and supervisors to become leaders and facilitators is another pitfall. It is management's duty to cultivate and nurture employees in order to reap the greatest benefits from their efforts. Establishing relationships and effective communication will allow employees to feel comfortable in relaying information back to management on quality issues that affect them. As employees become viewed as important assets in the organization, pride will continue to increase.

13. Inadequate Training

A reluctance to provide adequate training is a major pitfall that has become common in many organizations. Training and re-training needs to be emphasized as an important means of reaching total quality. Management also must support the process of training and retraining of existing employees in up-to-date techniques. This is a major component of continuous improvement, and must be realized before it can happen.

14. Failure to Support the Previous 13 Points

There must be a genuine commitment from management to embark on the journey to continuous improvement. A common pitfall occurs when overnight transformation is expected. Implementing organization-wide change cannot happen overnight. Patience and support will have to be given by top management if the process is to be successful. Living the steps to implement change is vital, and necessitates a long-term commitment.

CONCLUSION

As organizations are being thrust into the global marketplace, the quality of their goods and services will become a major factor in determining the longevity of their success. Organizations taking a retrenchment approach to quality are implementing their own demise. The challenges that are being presented by the global marketplace must be met with quick and decisive action. There will be no second chances in this highly competitive environment. Survival will boil down to innovative products that exceed customer expectations, even before the customer has them.[11]

There is no simple answer to meeting the challenge of implementing TQM successfully. Part of the solution is recognition by management that high quality can contribute significantly to bottom-line performance. Part is delivering high-quality needs that touch everyone in the organization and is not just limited to a Quality Assurance Department. Part of the answer lies in knowing that many steps will need to be taken to improve quality and that they need to be molded into a cohesive whole. Improving quality will require time, patience, and coordination. Most of all, it requires total commitment to the new philosophy. Anything else is managing for failure.

It needs to be emphasized that Deming's 14 points should be used as a road map, not a set of unquestionable rules cast in stone. Each organization will have to assess the validity of the 14 points using them as a guideline to tailor a system that is conducive to its particular organizational environment. Once this is realized, the organization can embark on the journey toward total quality by developing a quality system that will meet the organization's needs, as well as the needs of its customers.

REFERENCE NOTES

1. H. S. Gitlow and S. J. Gitlow, *The Deming Guide to Quality and Competitive Position.* 1987.

2. L. Schein, "The Culture of Service Quality," *Conference Board,* No. 963, 1991.

3. Gitlow and Gitlow, *op. cit.*

4. W. E. Deming, *Quality, Productivity and Competitive Position,* 1982.

5. K. D. Ryan and D. K. Oestreich, *Driving Fear Out of the Workplace,* San Francisco: Jossey Bass, 1991.

6. Deming, *op. cit.*

7. Gitlow and Gitlow, *op. cit.*

8. Deming, *op. cit.*

9. Deming, *op cit.*

10. Gitlow and Gitlow, *op. cit.*

11. R. E. Rogers, "Managing for Quality: A Comparison of Japanese and American Management Approaches," *National Productivity Review,* Autumn, 1993.

BIBLIOGRAPHY

Crosby, P. B., *Quality Is Free: The Art of Making Quality Certain.* New York: New American Library, 1979.

Deming, W. E., *Quality, Productivity and Competitive Position.* Cambridge, MA: Massachusetts Institute of Technology, Center for Advance Engineering Study, 1982.

Gitlow, H. S. and Gitlow, S. J., *The Deming Guide to Quality and Competitive Position.* Englewood Cliffs: NJ. Prentice Hall, 1987.

Houghton, J. R., "Leadership and Total Quality." Conference Board, 1990, *(Conference Board Report no. 937)*, p. 90.

Jacobsen, A. F., "Customer Expectations in the New Decade." *(Conference Board Report no. 963)*, 1991, p. 63.

Pfau, L. D., "Total Quality Management Gives Companies a Way to Enhance Position in Global Marketplace." *Industrial Engineering* 21 (no. 4), April 1989.

Rogers, R. E., "Managing for Quality: A Comparison of Japanese and American Management Approaches," *(National Productivity Review,* Autumn, 1993).

Ryan K. D., and Oestreich, D. K., "Driving Fear Out of the Workplace," San Francisco: Jossey Bass, 1991.

Schein, L., "The Road to Total Quality: Views of Industry Experts." *(Conference Board Research Bulletin no. 239)*, 1990, p. 17.

Schein, L., "The Culture of Service Quality" *(Conference Board Report no. 939)*, 1991, p. 63.

Wiggenhorn, W. A., "Creating Your Own Quality Definition." *(Conference Board Report no. 963)*, 1991, p. 63.

Chapter Three

TQM – Basic Concepts

TQM

TOTAL QUALITY MANAGEMENT IS
A CUSTOMER-ORIENTED, QUALITY-FOCUSED
MANAGEMENT PHILOSOPHY FOR
CONTINUOUS IMPROVEMENT.

TOTAL QUALITY MANAGEMENT

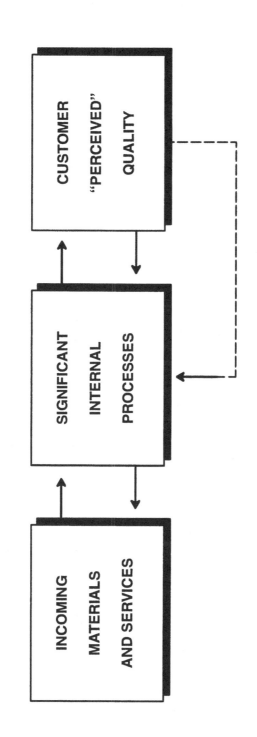

INCOMING MATERIALS AND SERVICES

SIGNIFICANT INTERNAL PROCESSES

CUSTOMER "PERCEIVED" QUALITY

Total Quality Management

TQM is the application of <u>quantitative methods</u> and <u>human resources</u> to assess and improve

- materials and services supplied to the organization;

- all significant processes within the organization; and

- meeting the needs of the customer, now and in the future.

THE CHAIN REACTION FOR QUALITY IMPROVEMENT

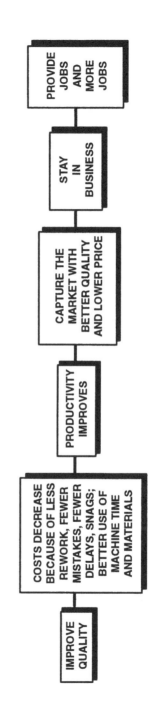

IMPROVE QUALITY

→

COSTS DECREASE BECAUSE OF LESS REWORK, FEWER MISTAKES, FEWER DELAYS, SNAGS; BETTER USE OF MACHINE TIME AND MATERIALS

→

PRODUCTIVITY IMPROVES

→

CAPTURE THE MARKET WITH BETTER QUALITY AND LOWER PRICE

→

STAY IN BUSINESS

→

PROVIDE JOBS AND MORE JOBS

Chapter Four

Planned Organizational Change

Defining the Future State

- Philosophy, mission, and values
- Expected organization structure
- Reward systems
- Personnel policies
- Authority and task/responsibility distributions
- Managerial styles
- Performance review systems
- Performance outcomes

IMPLEMENTING TOTAL QUALITY MANAGEMENT

CRITICAL MASS PHASE

MANAGEMENT EDUCATION

DEVELOP NEW QUALITY PHILOSOPHY

DEVELOP IMPLEMENTATION PLAN FOR
ESTABLISHMENT OF CRITICAL MASS

TRAIN MANAGEMENT AND STAFF

BEGIN INITIAL PROCESS IMPROVEMENT
EFFORTS

SOCIO-TECHNICAL CHANGE PHASE

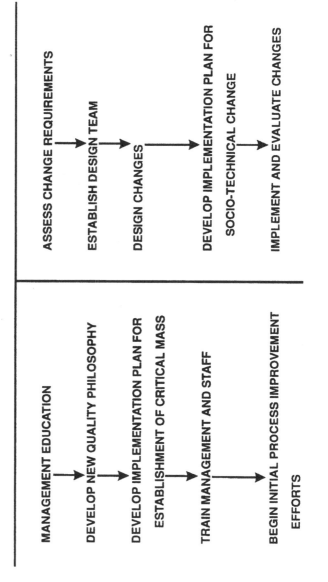

ASSESS CHANGE REQUIREMENTS

ESTABLISH DESIGN TEAM

DESIGN CHANGES

DEVELOP IMPLEMENTATION PLAN FOR
SOCIO-TECHNICAL CHANGE

IMPLEMENT AND EVALUATE CHANGES

Production Viewed as a <u>System</u>

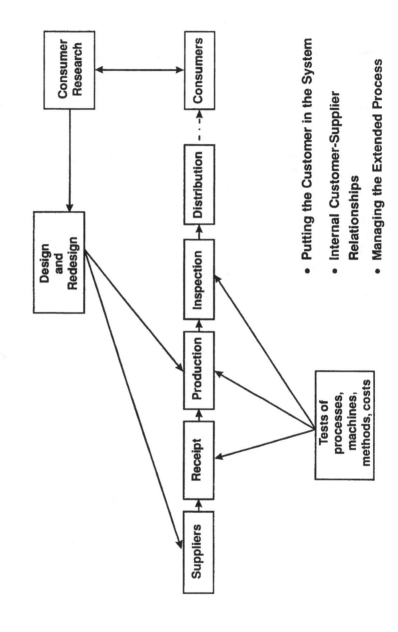

- Putting the Customer in the System
- Internal Customer-Supplier Relationships
- Managing the Extended Process

42

Chapter Five

A Management Structure for TQM

OUTLINE

- DEMING PRINCIPLES 8, 9, 12, 14

- CURRENT ORGANIZATIONAL STRUCTURE

- ORGANIZING FOR TRANSFORMATION

- PARALLEL STRUCTURE: WHO AND FUNCTION

- SUPPORT FUNCTIONS FOR TRANSFORMATION

44

IMPLEMENTING THE 14 MANAGEMENT PRINCIPLES

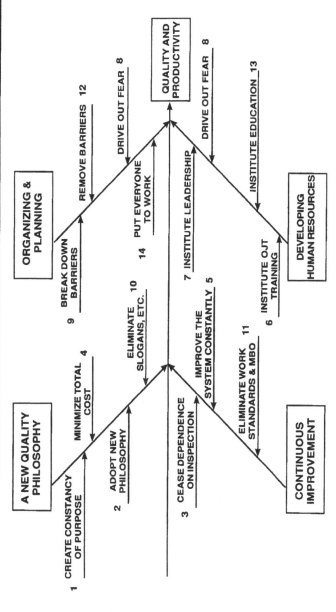

OUTLINE

- DEMING PRINCIPLES 8, 9, 12, 14

→ • CURRENT ORGANIZATIONAL STRUCTURE

- ORGANIZING FOR TRANSFORMATION

- PARALLEL STRUCTURE: WHO AND FUNCTION

- SUPPORT FUNCTIONS FOR TRANSFORMATION

TYPICAL HIERARCHICAL ORGANIZATION

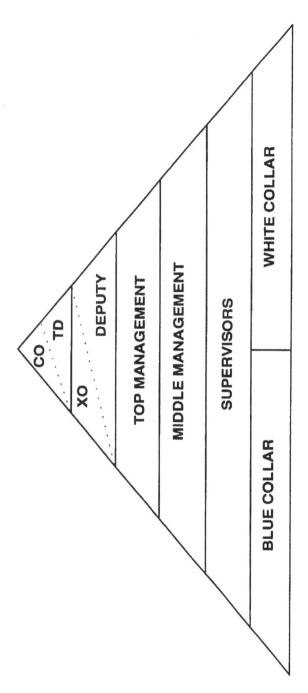

CO
TD
XO
DEPUTY
TOP MANAGEMENT
MIDDLE MANAGEMENT
SUPERVISORS
BLUE COLLAR
WHITE COLLAR

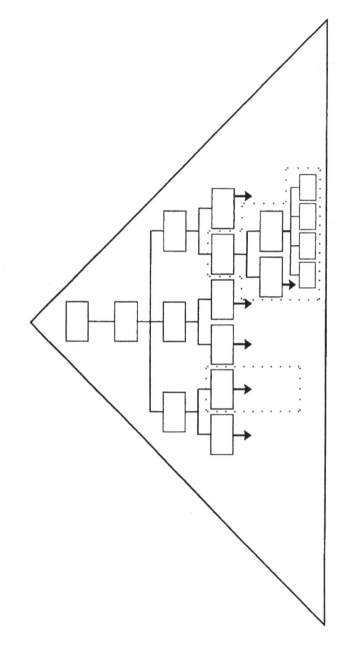

BARRIERS TO IMPROVEMENT

48

OUTLINE

- DEMING PRINCIPLES 8, 9, 12, 14

- CURRENT ORGANIZATIONAL STRUCTURE

- ORGANIZING FOR TRANSFORMATION

- PARALLEL STRUCTURE: WHO AND FUNCTION

- SUPPORT FUNCTIONS FOR TRANSFORMATION

49

MANAGING FOR QUALITY

- CUSTOMER-ORIENTED

- PROCESS-ORIENTED/CROSS-FUNCTIONAL

- INVOLVES ALL ORGANIZATIONAL LEVELS

- FACILITATES TOP-DOWN MANAGEMENT

- LINKED FOR COMMUNICATION AND DECISION MAKING

- FOLLOWS THE CHAIN OF COMMAND

- TRANSITIONAL

ORGANIZATION OF QUALITY MANAGEMENT

- EXECUTIVE STEERING COMMITTEE (ESC)

- QUALITY MANAGEMENT BOARDS (QMBS)

- PROCESS ACTION TEAMS (PATS)

OUTLINE

- DEMING PRINCIPLES 8, 9, 12, 14

- CURRENT ORGANIZATIONAL STRUCTURE

- ORGANIZING FOR TRANSFORMATION

→ • PARALLEL STRUCTURE: WHO AND FUNCTION

- SUPPORT FUNCTIONS FOR TRANSFORMATION

QUESTIONS

1. WHO PARTICIPATES IN EACH GROUP?

2. WHEN IS EACH GROUP ESTABLISHED?

3. WHAT IS THE FUNCTION OF EACH GROUP?

4. HOW DO THE GROUPS RELATE TO ONE ANOTHER?

5. HOW DO THE GROUPS RELATE TO PROCESS IMPROVEMENT?

MANAGEMENT OF PROCESS IMPROVEMENT

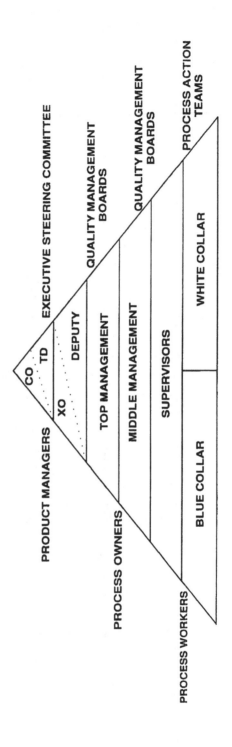

EXECUTIVE STEERING COMMITTEE (ESC)

WHO

- TOP LEVEL MANAGEMENT

FUNCTION

- IDENTIFIES EXTERNAL CUSTOMER REQUIREMENTS

- DEVELOPS QUALITY MANAGEMENT PHILOSOPHY

- DEVELOPS TQM STRATEGIC PLAN

- REMOVES IMPEDIMENTS TO THE PHILOSOPHY AND PLAN

- IDENTIFIES PROCESSES AND CHARTERS QMBS

- PROVIDES RESOURCES AND DECISION SUPPORT TO QMBS

- ESTABLISHES POSITIONS TO SUPPORT THE QUALITY TRANSFORMATION

QUALITY MANAGEMENT BOARD (QMB)

WHO

- PROCESS OWNERS (MIDDLE MANAGEMENT) CHARTERED BY THE ESC

FUNCTION

- DEVELOPS PLANS FOR PROCESS IMPROVEMENT

- INITIATES PROCESS ANALYSIS

- CHARTERS PROCESS ACTION TEAMS TO WORK ON <u>SUB-PROCESS</u> AND COLLECT DATA

- EVALUATES EFFECTS OF PROCESS CHANGES

- RECOMMENDS MAJOR PROCESS CHANGES TO ESC

- PROVIDES RESOURCES AND DECISION SUPPORT TO PATS

PROCESS ACTION TEAM (PAT)

WHO

- PROCESS WORKERS CHARTERED BY THE QMB

FUNCTION

- DEVELOPS MEASURES

- ESTABLISHES DATA COLLECTION PROCEDURES

- IDENTIFIES AND REMOVES SPECIAL CAUSES OF VARIATION

- MAKES RECOMMENDATIONS FOR REDUCING COMMON CAUSE OF VARIATION

- DOCUMENTS PROCESS ANALYSIS AND IMPROVEMENT ACTIVITIES

QUESTIONS

1. WHO PARTICIPATES IN EACH GROUP?

2. WHEN IS EACH GROUP ESTABLISHED?

3. WHAT IS THE FUNCTION OF EACH GROUP?

4. HOW DO THE GROUPS RELATE TO ONE ANOTHER?

5. HOW DO THE GROUPS RELATE TO PROCESS IMPROVEMENT?

LINKING FOR COMMUNICATION AND DECISION MAKING

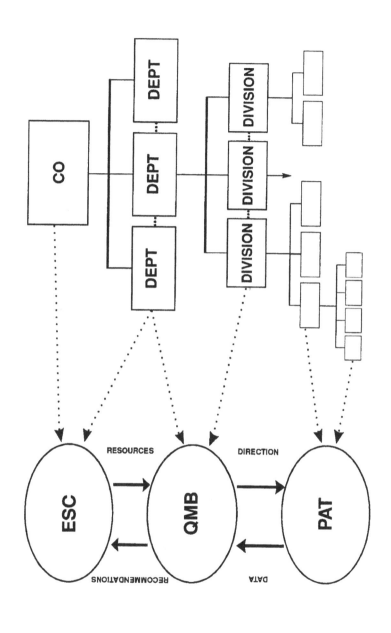

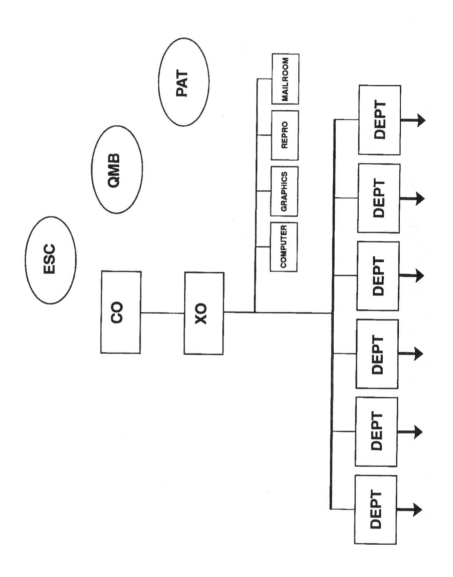

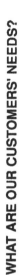

- WHAT ARE OUR CUSTOMERS' NEEDS?
- WHAT ARE OUR CRITICAL PROCESSES?
- DO OUR PROCESSES MEET CUSTOMERS' NEEDS?
- WHAT CHANGES ARE REQUIRED FOR QUALITY IMPROVEMENT?

- HOW DOES THE PROCESS WORK?
- WHICH PROCESS VARIABLES ARE MOST SIGNIFICANT FOR QUALITY?
- HOW DO WE GATHER BASELINE DATA?
- WHAT RESOURCES ARE NEEDED TO ANALYZE/IMPROVE THE PROCESS?

- HOW DO WE FURTHER ANALYZE THE PROCESS?
- CAN WE CONDUCT A TEST?
- WHAT DID WE LEARN FROM THE DATA COLLECTED?
- ARE THERE SPECIAL CAUSES TO BE CORRECTED?

ESC

QMB

PAT

RESOURCES

DIRECTION

DATA

RECOMMENDATIONS

Chapter Six

TQM
Education and Training

IMPLEMENTING THE 14 MANAGEMENT PRINCIPLES

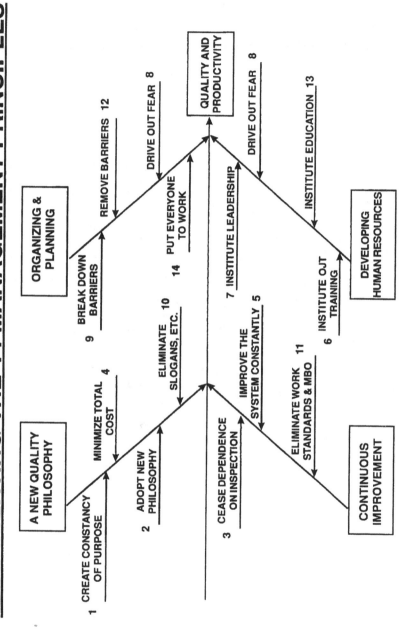

EDUCATION AND TRAINING

PRINCIPLE 13: INSTITUTE A VIGOROUS PROGRAM OF EDUCATION AND SELF-IMPROVEMENT

PRINCIPLE 6: INSTITUTE TRAINING ON THE JOB

65

TQM EDUCATION AND TRAINING ISSUES

- MAKE OR BUY
- ESTABLISH IN-HOUSE CAPABILITY
  - DEVELOPING CURRICULUM
  - IDENTIFYING AND TRAINING TRAINERS
  - EXPANSION AND UPDATE
  - CONSISTENCY OF CONCEPTS, APPROACHES, AND LANGUAGE
  - INTEGRATION WITH EXISTING CURRICULUM
- RESOURCES AND SUPPORT
- TRAINING SEQUENCE-SUBJECTS AND PARTICIPANTS

TQM EDUCATION AND TRAINING APPROACHES

- EDUCATION PRECEDES TRAINING

- TOP-DOWN

- INTEGRATED WITH IMPLEMENTATION PLAN

- JUST-IN-TIME

- TEAM TRAINING

- COMPREHENSIVE COVERAGE (CURRICULUM AND PEOPLE)

- ONGOING

67

WHO SHOULD BE "EDUCATED" AND IN WHAT ORDER

- NEAR-TERM (THE "CRITICAL MASS")

  – KEY PERSONNEL INVOLVED IN IMPLEMENTATION (ESC, QMBs, PATs)

  – DEVELOPERS AND PROVIDERS OF E & T

  – TQM COORDINATORS AND STATISTICIANS

- MID-TERM

  – MID- AND LOWER MANAGEMENT

- LONG-TERM

  – EVERYONE IN THE ORGANIZATION

EDUCATION AND TRAINING STRATEGY FOR TQM

LEVEL
III
ADVANCED
METHODS

LEVEL
II
BASIC
METHODS

LEVEL I
TOTAL QUALITY THEORY
AND BASIC CONCEPTS

LEVEL I: THEORY AND BASIC CONCEPTS

- ORGANIZATION VIEWED AS A SYSTEM

- CONTROL VS QUALITY MANAGEMENT

- THE CHAIN REACTION OF QUALITY AND PRODUCTIVITY

- THE PARADIGM SHIFT

- CONTINUOUS IMPROVEMENT

- PROCESS ANALYSIS, CONTROL, AND IMPROVEMENT

- VARIATION: COMMON AND SPECIAL CAUSES

- CUSTOMER ORIENTATION

- CROSS-FUNCTIONAL MANAGEMENT TEAMS

LEVEL II: BASIC METHODS AND TOOLS

- INTRODUCTION TO THE SCIENTIFIC METHOD
  - ROLE OF MEASUREMENT
  - BASELINING; PRE-POST; SUBGROUPING

- STATISTICAL THINKING
  - ENUMERATIVE VS ANALYTIC STUDIES
  - SPECIAL VS COMMON CAUSES
  - TAGUCHI LOSS FUNCTION

- BASIC GRAPHIC TOOLS
  - THE SEVEN BASIC TOOLS
  - THE SEVEN "NEW" TOOLS
  - PROCESS CAPABILITY
  - CONTROL CHART PATTERNS

- OTHER ANALYTIC METHODS
  - PROCESS IMPROVEMENT MODEL
  - GROUP PROCESS AND DECISION MAKING

LEVEL III: ADVANCED METHODS

- ADVANCED SCIENTIFIC METHODOLOGY

- QUALITY FUNCTION DEPLOYMENT

- OFF-LINE EXPERIMENTAL METHODS

- SOCIO-TECHNICAL REDESIGN

72

COURSES

TRAINEE GROUPS	AWARENESS	LEVEL I THEORY & CONCEPTS	LEVEL II PROCESS IMPROVEMENT	LEVEL II STATISTICAL TOOLS	LEVEL II PLANNING TOOLS	LEADING TEAMS	TEAM FUNCTION (GROUP SKILLS)	IMPLEMENTATION	LEVEL III ADVANCED METHODS
TOP MANAGEMENT	1	2		4			3		
MIDDLE MANAGEMENT	1	3	5	4	6	7			
SUPERVISORS	1	2	3		4				
EMPLOYEES	1					4			
TQM COORDINATOR	1	4	5	6			3		
STATISTICIAN	1	3	4					5	
STATISTICAL TECH./TRAINER	1	4	5	6	7	8	3	9	
TEAMS	1	2	3			4			

Chapter Seven

Organization Assessment

What Is It?

- A methodology to:

  – Assess readiness for change

    Identify strengths and weaknesses

  – Determine action

  – Measure effectiveness of efforts

  – Monitor organization-wide progress

- A continuous requirement

Why Do It?

- TQM requires strategic (long-term) planning

- Assessment is an integral part of planning

- Provides data to help direct change

- Provides information to assess degree of change

FUNCTIONS OF AN ORGANIZATION-WIDE SURVEY
(Generic)

- Gathers information for a <u>purpose</u>

- Provides data to take action

- Diagnoses employees' knowledge, attitudes, and perceptions concerning their workplace

- Establishes a <u>baseline</u> for future comparisons

- Provides two-way communication between managers and employees

- Provides avenue for employee participation

- Indicates avenue for employee participation

- Raises expectations

When Do You Do It?

- Needs assessment (baseline)

- Periodic intervals (annually)

- Forever

How Is It Done?

- Introduce purpose/planned use

- Interview/questionnaire

- Existing data bases (local)

- Paper and pencil vs automated

- Self-assessment vs external assistance

- Survey feedback methods/focus groups

What Is Measured?

- Management leadership

- Management practices and involvement

- Employee involvement/perceptions/attitudes

- Teamwork

- Recognition systems

- Training requirements

- Process improvement activities

- Use of statistical methods/tools

Who Participates?

- Everyone in the organization

- Different perspectives

  - Top managers

  - Middle level managers

  - Supervisors

  - Work force

- A profile of organizational climate

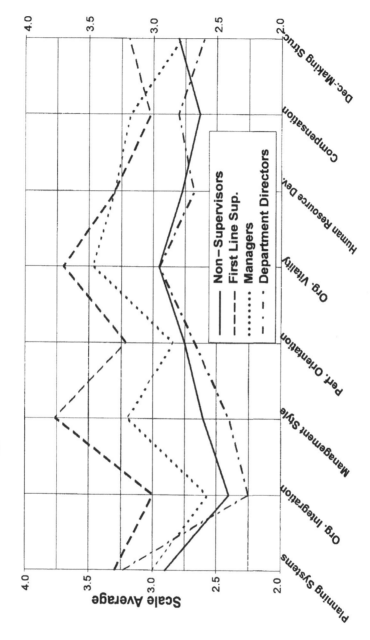

Organization Climate Profile

Scale Average

Legend:
- Non–Supervisors
- First Line Sup.
- Managers
- Department Directors

X-axis categories: Dec.-Making Struc., Compensation, Human Resource Dev., Org. Vitality, Perf. Orientation, Management Style, Org. Integration, Planning Systems

Chapter Eight

TQM Implementation Guidelines

INITIAL MEETINGS OF TQM CONSULTANT WITH CO AND SELECTED MANAGERS.

TQM ORIENTATION MEETINGS WITH CO, TQM CONSULTANT, AND ALL OF THE TOP MANAGERS.

BASIC TQM CONCEPTS (LEVEL I) TRAINING FOR TOP MANAGERS BEGINS.

INCUBATION AND DISCUSSION OF TQM; DETERMINATION OF STRATEGIC IMPLICATIONS.

EXECUTIVE STEERING COMMITTEE FORMED.

TQM COORDINATOR ROLE DEFINED;
COORDINATOR SELECTED AND TRAINED.

TQM POLICY SPECIFIED BY TOP MANAGEMENT

TQM IMPLEMENTERS' SEMINAR CONDUCTED BY
TQM CONSULTANT (AT THE DIRECTION OF THE
ESC).

IMPLEMENTATION PLANNING BY THE ESC BEGINS.

BASIC CONCEPTS (LEVEL I) TRAINING FOR MIDDLE MANAGERS BEGINS.

ORGANIZATION ASSESSMENT.

MIDDLE MANAGEMENT WORKSHOPS FOR POLICY DEPLOYMENT.

SELECTION OF PROCESS IMPROVEMENT PROTOTYPES.

DETERMINE CUSTOMER REQUIREMENTS.

CHARTERING OF QUALITY MANAGEMENT BOARDS.

SELECTION AND TRAINING OF TQM TRAINERS.

START TRAINING TEAM LEADERS.

SELECTION AND TRAINING OF FIRST PROCESS ACTION TEAMS.

ESC ACTIONS IN PREPARATION FOR PHASE II IMPLEMENTATION.

REFINE IMPLEMENTATION PLANS.

ESC OVERSEES PROCESS IMPROVEMENT PROTOTYPES.

DEVELOP ONGOING CAPABILITY FOR LEVEL I TRAINING.

START TRAINING GENERAL (NON-SUPERVISORY) PERSONNEL.

EXPAND EFFORTS TO INCLUDE EXTERNAL SUPPLIERS AND CUSTOMERS.

Chapter Nine

A Total Quality Management Process Improvement Model

IMPLEMENTING THE 14 MANAGEMENT PRINCIPLES

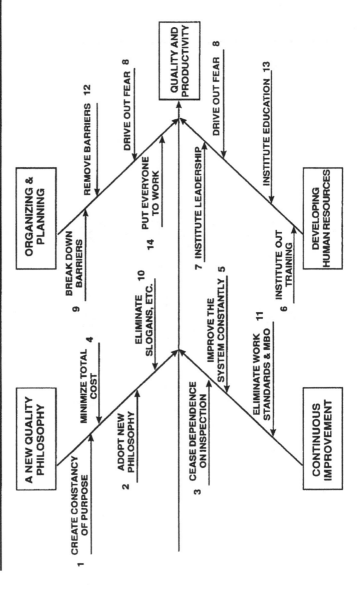

PURPOSE

- To identify roles in process improvement

- To define the activities required to perform the Process Improvement Model (PIM)

- To give an overview of basic statistical process control (SPC) methods associated with process analysis and improvement.

SOME IMPROVEMENT PREREQUISITES

- Customer's needs and wants

- Organizational system

- Long-range strategic planning (mission, values, and beliefs)

- Organizational assessment

- Education and training

- Organizational structure (roles and responsibilities)

THE SHEWHART CYCLE

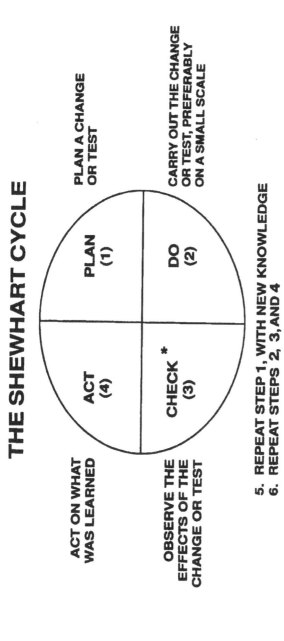

PLAN A CHANGE
OR TEST

CARRY OUT THE CHANGE
OR TEST, PREFERABLY
ON A SMALL SCALE

PLAN
(1)

DO
(2)

ACT
(4)

CHECK *
(3)

ACT ON WHAT
WAS LEARNED

OBSERVE THE
EFFECTS OF THE
CHANGE OR TEST

5. REPEAT STEP 1, WITH NEW KNOWLEDGE
6. REPEAT STEPS 2, 3, AND 4

*Stage 3 was later changed to "Study" by Deming.
Note: The concept above was originated by Walter A. Shewhart, *Statistical Method from the Viewpoint of Quality Control* (Graduate School, Department of Agriculture, Washington, 1939; Dover 1986), p. 45. Deming called it (in Japan in 1950 and thereafter) the Shewhart cycle. It went into immediate use in Japan under the name "Deming cycle," and this name has been used there ever since.

USE OF "PLAN-DO-CHECK-ACT" CYCLE

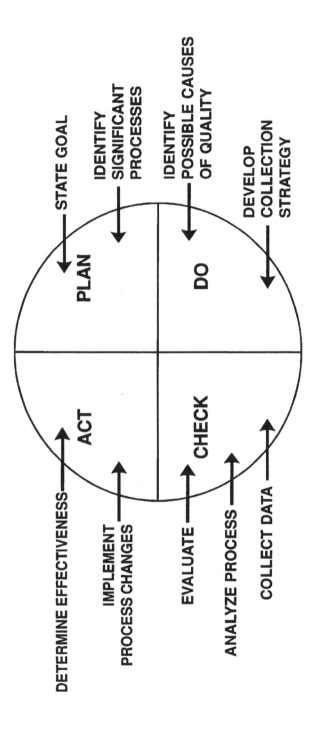

RESPONSIBILITIES DURING THE IMPROVEMENT CYCLE

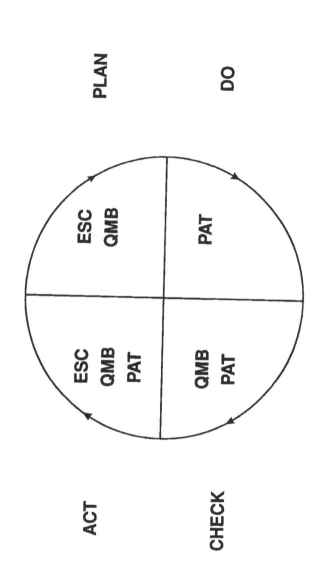

PLAN

DO

ACT

CHECK

ESC
QMB

PAT

ESC
QMB
PAT

QMB
PAT

PROCESS IMPROVEMENT MODEL FOR TOTAL QUALITY MANAGEMENT

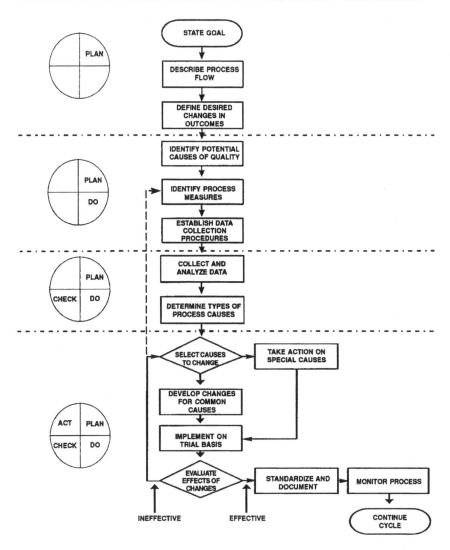

TRANSLATING THE VOICE OF THE CUSTOMER

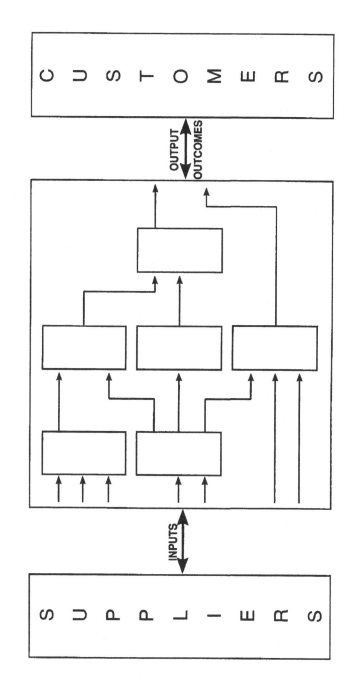

PROCESS IMPROVEMENT MODEL FOR TOTAL QUALITY MANAGEMENT

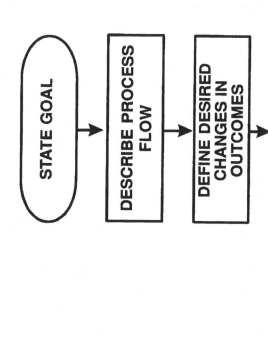

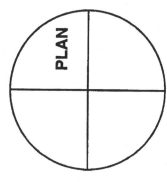

PLAN PHASE (ESC and QMB Responsibility)

- Involves identifying and defining critical product and service requirements of customers

- Requires the prioritization of goals

- Provides a focus and scope for improvement efforts

PROCESS IMPROVEMENT MODEL (Cont.)

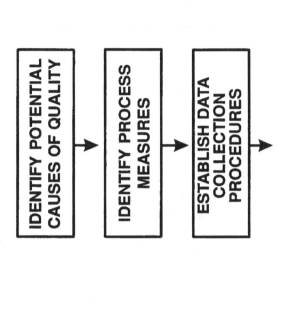

IDENTIFY POTENTIAL CAUSES OF QUALITY

IDENTIFY PROCESS MEASURES

ESTABLISH DATA COLLECTION PROCEDURES

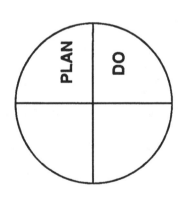

PLAN

DO

102

PROCESS IMPROVEMENT MODEL (Cont.)

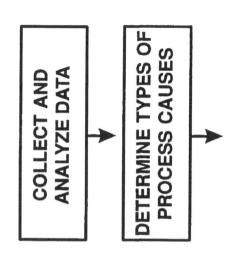

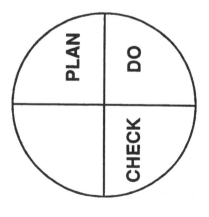

PROCESS IMPROVEMENT MODEL (Cont.)

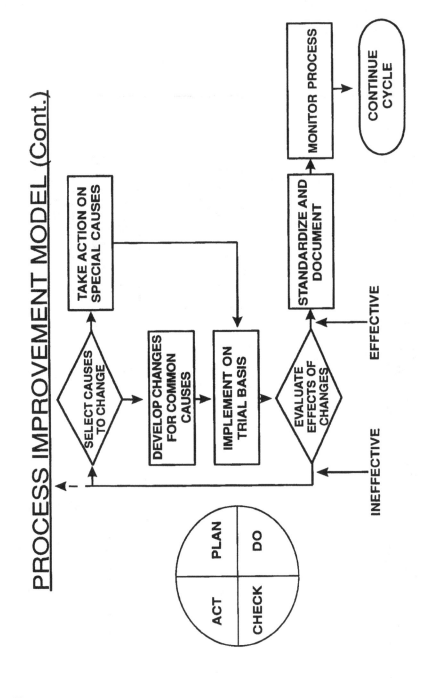

BASIC GRAPHIC TOOLS

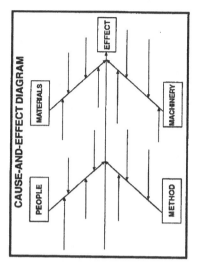

CAUSE-AND-EFFECT DIAGRAM

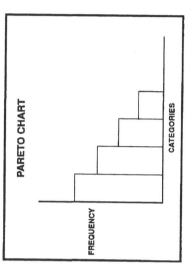

PARETO CHART

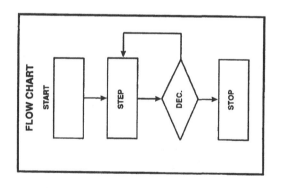

FLOW CHART

BASIC GRAPHIC TOOLS (Cont.)

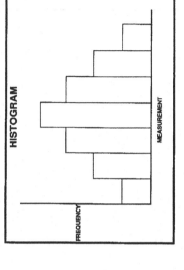

SCATTER DIAGRAM

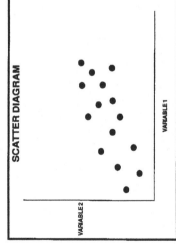

HISTOGRAM

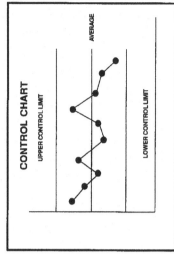

CONTROL CHART

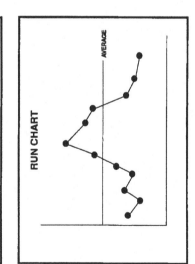

RUN CHART

CONTINUE THE CYCLE

- Select new goal

  -- At the organizational level: select from list of customer concerns

  -- At the process level: follow up on findings of previous process improvement efforts

Selected Books and Monographs

The amount of material being published, literally daily, in quality management and related subjects has become profuse. The following selected references are either classics or were current at the time of publication of this book. Announcements of new material are issued periodically by professional associations such as the ones listed in the *Selected Quality Management Journals* section below.

Aguayo, R., *Dr. Deming, the American Who Taught the Japanese About Quality.* New York: Carol Publishing, 1990.

Bockerstette, J. and Shell, R., *Time Based Manufacturing.* Available through IE&M Press, #716B.

Bowles, J. and Hammond, J., *Beyond Quality: How 50 Winning Companies Use Continuous Improvement.* New York: Putnam, 1991.

Brown, M. G., *Baldrige Award-Winning Quality.* Available through ASQC Quality Press, #H0802.

Camp, R., *Bench Marketing.* Available through IE&M Press, #650B.

Cartin, T., *Principles and Practices of TQM.* Available through ASQC Quality Press, #H0691.

Cocheu, T., *Making Quality Happen.* San Francisco: Jossey-Bass, 1993.

Crosby, P., *Quality Is Free.* New York: Mentor, 1979.

Crosby, P., *Quality Without Tears: The Art Of Hassle-Free Management.* New York: McGraw Hill 1984.

Deming, W.E., *Out of The Crisis,* Cambridge, MA: MIT, 1982.

Feigenbaum, A. *Total Quality Control.* New York: McGraw Hill, 1983.

Gitlow, H. S. and Gitlow, S. J. *The Deming Guide to Quality and Competitive Position.* Englewood Cliffs, NJ: Prentice-Hall, 1987.

Gitlow, H., *Planning For Quality, Productivity, and Competitive Position.* Homewood, Il: Dow Jones-Irwin, 1990.

Gogg, T. and Mott, J., *Improve Quality and Productivity with Simulation.* Available through IE&M Press, #706B.

Harrington, H., *Business Process Improvement.* New York: McGraw-Hill, 1991.

Hackman, J. R. and Oldham, G. R., *Work Redesign.* Available through AQP #AW08P.

Hall, S., *Quality Assurance in the Hospitality Industry.* Available through ASQC Quality Press, #H0602.

Harrington, H., *Business Process Improvement.* New York: McGraw-Hill, 1991.

Imai, M., *KAIZEN: The Key to Japan's Success.* New York: Random House, 1986.

ISO 9004 Guidelines. Geneva, Switzerland, 1987.

Juran, J. M., *Juran On Leadership For Quality.* New York: Free Press, 1989.

Juran, J. M., *Juran's Quality Control Handbook* (4th edition). New York: McGraw-Hill, 1988.

Monden, Y., *Toyota Production System* (2nd edition). Available through: IE&M Press, #127B.

Omahonu, V., *Total Quality And Productivity Management In Health Care Organizations.* Available through: IE&M Press, #744B.

Parker, G., *Team Players and Team Work.* San Francisco: Jossey-Bass, 1990.

Peters, T., *Thriving On Chaos.* New York: Knopf, 1988.

Ross, P., *Taguchi Techniques For Quality Engineering.* New York: McGraw-Hill, 1988.

Ryan K., and Oestreich, D., *Driving Fear Out of the Workplace.* Available from AQP, #JB24H.

Scholtes, P., *The Team Handbook.* Madison, WI: Joiner Associates, 1990.

Schuster, D., *Teaming for Quality Improvement.* Englewood Cliffs, NJ: Prentice-Hall, 1990.

Spanbauer, S., *A Quality System for Education.* Available through ASQC Quality Press, #H0694.

Walton, M., *Deming Management at Work.* Available through ASQC Quality Press #H0635.

Westland, C. L., *Quality: The Myth and the Magic.* Available through ASQC Quality Press, #H0606.

Wollschlaeger L., *The Quality Promise.* New York: Marcel Dekker, 1990.

SELECTED QUALITY MANAGEMENT JOURNALS

Publisher	Publications
American Society for Quality Control P. O. Box 3005 Milwaukee,WI 53201-3005	*Quality Progress* *Journal of Quality Technology*
Marcel Dekker, Inc. 270 Madison Avenue New York, NY 10016	*Quality Engineering*
Executive Enterprises Publications 22 West 21st Street New York, NY 10010-6904	*National Productivity Review*
Institute of Industrial Engineers 25 Technology Park/Atlanta Norcross, GA 30092-2988	*Industrial Engineering*
The Quality Observer P. O. Box 1111 Fairfax, VA 22032	*The Quality Observer*

Index

Aguayo, R., 109
Allied-Signal Corp., 7
AMA. *See* American Medical
    Association
American Medical Association,
    10,11
American Society for Quality
    Control, 112
Ameritech, 10
AT&T, 10
Authority
  lines of, 27
  and managers, 27
Auto industry, 3-7
Auto quality, 13

Barriers in organization, 21
  barriers to improvement, chart, 48
  between departments, 21
  breakdown of, 2,21
  due to lack of communication, 21
  effects of, 2
  employee resistance to removing,
    28
  management removal of, 24,25
  reasons for, 21
  rob employees of pride, 22
Bockerstette, J., 109
Bowles, J., 109
B. P. American, 9
Brown, M. G., 109
Buin and Company, 8

Cadillac, 4,6
Camp, R., 109
Cartin, T., 109

Chrysler, 4
Cocheu, T., 109
Colgate Palmolive Company, 3
Commitment to quality, 4
Communication
  effective communication, 29
  linking for decision making chart,
    59
  organizational communication, 27
  posters and slogans, 28
  training in, 23
Concurrent engineering, 5
  defined, 6
Constancy of purpose, 4,16,64
Continue the cycle, chart, 107
Continuous improvement, 15
  of the system, 18,21,64
Critical mass phase, 41,68
Crosby, P., 13,32,109,110
Customer(s)
  relationship with in service
    industries, 7,8
  responsiveness to, 17
  retention, 8
  voice of, 99
Cycle-time, 5

Defect detection, 17,25
Defect prevention, 17
Defects, auto industry, 4
Deming, W. E., 1,2,3,12,13,31,
    32,110
Deming's 14 Points, 2,15-24
  implementing 14 principles,
    charts, 45,64
Design, benefits of quality design, 6

Design-for-manufacturing, 6
Developing human resources, chart,
    92

Education
    of employees, 8,9,23
    importance of, 23
    TQM education and training
        issues, charts, 66-69
    and training, 23
    and training, chart, 65
Employee
    as assets to organization, 19,22
    customer contact with, 9
    making decisions, 9
    pride, 23
    retraining, 9
    training in quality awareness, 17
Empowering workers, 3
Executive Enterprises Publications,
    112
Executive steering committee (ESC),
    chart, 55

Fear
    driving out fear, 20,28
    in the workplace, 20
    moving from status quo, 17
    monitoring fear, 27
    related to quotas, 22
Federal Express, 9
Feigenbaum, A., 110
Ford (motor company), 4,10
Future state, defined, 40

General Electric, 9
Gitlow, H., 13,14,31,32,110
Gitlow, S., 13,14,31,32,110
GM (General Motors), 4,5
Godfrey, A. B., 10
Gogg, T., 110

Graphic tools, 105-106
    cause-and-effect diagram, 105
    control chart, 106
    flow chart, 105
    histogram, 106
    pareto chart, 105
    run chart, 106
    scatter diagram, 106
Goals
    and continuous improvement
        of quality, 21
    eliminating unproductive goals, 21
    long-term, 4,16
    numerical goals and their use, 28
    organizational, 16
    qualitative vs. quantitative, 29
    short-term, 4,16
    strategic, 4
    unifying goals, 16

Hackman, J. R., 110
Hall, S., 110
Hammond, J., 109
Harrington, H., 110
Hart, D. K., 14
Health care industry, 9-12
    consistency in care, 9
    customers in, 10
    product in, 10
    suppliers in, 10
Health maintenance organizations
    (HMOs), 10-11
Healthcare Inc., 11
Heinze Company, 2
Hewlett-Packard, 10
Hill Pet Products Inc., 3
HMOs. *See* Health maintenance
    organizations
Houghton, J. R., 32
Huthwait, B., 13

Imai, M., 110
Improvement cycle, 97
Industrial Engineering, 112

Intermountain Health Care Inc.
(IHC), 11
Interstudy, 10
Institute for Healthcare Delivery, 11
Institute of Industrial Engineers, 112

Jacobsen, A. F., 32
James, B. C., 11
Journal of Quality Technology, 112
Journey to quality, 16
Juran, J. M., 12,110
Juran Institute Inc., 10
Just-in-time systems, 5

Kodak, 2

Lapp, G. D., 1
Liswood, L., 13

3M, 2
Malcom Baldridge National Quality
Award, 4
Management
ability to define quality, 25
evaluation of quality, 28-29
as facilitators, 24,29
failure to provide adequate
training, 26,30
failure to provide supportive
atmosphere, 26
Fourteen Management Principles,
45
as leaders, 29
lines of authority, 27
as planners, 24
relationship to vendors, 25-26
removing fears, 25
responsibility in removing
barriers, 24-25,28
responsibility to vendors, 25-26

Management *(continued)*
and TQM implementation, 24-32
views into the future, 24,29
Managing for quality, chart, 50
Marcel Dekker, Inc., 112
Marriott Corp., 9,10
Mass inspection, 17
Mission statement, 4
as "guide" for the organization,
16
development and importance
of, 16
necessity to keep it flexible, 24
as a set of beliefs, 24
Monden, Y., 110
Motorola, 11
Mott, J., 110

National Demonstration Project
on Quality Improvement
in Health Care, 110
National Productivity Review, 112

Oestreich, D. K., 31,32,110
Oldham, G. R., 110
Omahonu, V., 110
Organization. *See* Organizational
assessment, chart, 75-83
assessment, defined, 76
climate profile, chart, 83
how to assess, chart, 80
survey functions, chart, 78
what to assess, chart, 81
when to assess, chart, 79
who participates in assessment, 82
Organizational. *See* Organization
change, planned, 39
climate, 83
commitment to change, 30
culture, 16
flexibility, 24
goals, 16
hierarchical organization, chart, 47
philosophy, 16,17,24

Organizational *(continued)*
  pitfalls due to poor leadership, 29
  planned organizational change,
    charts, 39-42

Parker, G., 110
Parker Hannifin Company, 9
PAT, 61. *See* Process action team
Peters, T., 110
Pfau, L. D., 32
Pitfalls for management, 24-32
"Plan-do-check-act" cycle, 96
Plan phase, 101
Planning chart, 77
Powers, J. D. and Associates, 4
Price-tag and purchasing, 18
Pride
  importance of employee pride,
    22,23,30
  inappropriate instilling of pride,
    29
  increasing pride, 30
Problem-solving
  six-steps technique, 5
  problem solving skills, 17
Process action team (PAT), chart, 57
Process improvement, 54,93
Process improvement model (PIM)
    charts, 91-104
  management of process
    improvement, chart, 54
  plan-do-check-act phase, 104
  plan-do-check phase, 103
  plan-do-phase, 102
  plan phase, 100
Production, as a system, 42
Productivity, defined, 1
Purchasing, 18
  from multiple vendors, 18
  and price, 18
  purchasing agents, 18

Quality
  awareness, 17

Quality *(continued)*
  how to define, 25
  improvement, 37
  organization of quality
    management, chart, 51
Quality Engineering, 112
Quality management board (QMB)
    charts, 56,61
Quality Observer, The, 112
Quality Progress, 112
Quotas
  disadvantages of, 22
  effects on consumers, 22
  effects on employees, 22
  quota systems, 22

Reichheld, F., 8
Reliance Electric Company, 9
Responsiveness to customers, 17
Retention rate of customers, 8
Retraining, 23. *See* Training
    employees
Rogers, R. E., vi,14,32
Ross, P., 111
Ryan, K. D., 31,32,111

Schein, L., 31,32
Scholtes, P., 111
Schuster, D., 111
Scott, W. G., 14
Self-improvement of employees, 8,9
Services industries, 7-9
Shell, R., 109
Shewhart Cycle, 95
Shortell, S., 11
Short-term vs. long-term view, 16
Simplicity, 5-7
Simplifying operations, 6
Socio-technical change phase, 41
Spanbauer, S., 111
Stashower, L., 11
Statistical process control (SPC), 93
Statistics
  use of, 25

Statistics *(continued)*
  in vendor relationships, 25
Supervision of employees, 19-20,27
  aims of, 20
  benefits of, 20
  use of control charts in, 20

Tackitt, S., 15
Teamwork. *See* Workteams
  auto industry, 4-5
Total Quality Management.
    See TQM
TQM
  basic concepts, 33-38
  continuous improvement in, 23
  courses in training, chart, 74
  customer service in, 8
  implementation, 14
  implementation guidelines, charts,
    86-90
  implementing TQM, chart, 41
  inadequate training in, 30
  levels of training, charts, 70-72
  management responsibility
    in, 19,20
  management structure, 43
  TQM, charts, 33-38

TQM *(continued)*
  TQM education and training
    issues, charts, 66-69
  training employees in, 8,19,20
  training on the job, 19

University Microfilms Inc., 9
University of Michigan Hospital, 10

Vendors
  multiple, 18
  single vs. multiple, 25

Walton, M., 111
Westland, C. L., 111
Wiggenhorn, W. A., 32
Wollschlaeger, L., 111
Workers
  empowering, 3
  improving morale in, 3
Work standards, 22
Workmanship, 22
Workteams, 3
  in auto industry, 4

Xerox Corporation, 10

Printed in the United States
by Baker & Taylor Publisher Services